ALL AROUND THE WORLD
CANADA

by Jessica Dean

D1415068

Ideas for Parents and Teachers

Pogo Books let children practice reading informational text while introducing them to nonfiction features such as headings, labels, sidebars, maps, and diagrams, as well as a table of contents, glossary, and index.

Carefully leveled text with a strong photo match offers early fluent readers the support they need to succeed.

Before Reading

- "Walk" through the book and point out the various nonfiction features. Ask the student what purpose each feature serves.
- Look at the glossary together. Read and discuss the words.

Read the Book

- Have the child read the book independently.
- Invite him or her to list questions that arise from reading.

After Reading

- Discuss the child's questions. Talk about how he or she might find answers to those questions.
- Prompt the child to think more. Ask: Lumber is an important export of Canada. It makes paper products. What paper products do you use?

Pogo Books are published by Jump!
5357 Penn Avenue South
Minneapolis, MN 55419
www.jumplibrary.com

Library of Congress Cataloging-in-Publication Data

Names: Dean, Jessica, 1963– author.
Title: Canada / by Jessica Dean.
Description: Pogo books edition. | Minneapolis : Jump!, Inc., [2018] | Series: All around the world | Includes index.
Audience: Ages 7–10.
Identifiers: LCCN 2017050307 (print) | LCCN 2017051415 (ebook) | ISBN 9781624968952 (hardcover : alk. paper) | ISBN 9781624968969 (pbk.) | ISBN 9781624968976 (ebook)
Subjects: LCSH: Canada–Juvenile literature.
Classification: LCC F1008.2 .D385 2018 (print) | LCC F1008.2 (ebook) | DDC 971–dc23
LC record available at https://lccn.loc.gov/2017050307

Editor: Kristine Spanier
Book Designer: Leah Sanders

Photo Credits: Lucky-photographer/Shutterstock, cover; Javen/Shutterstock, 1; Pixfiction/Shutterstock, 3; Michael Wheatley/Getty, 4; RichardSeeley/iStock, 5; Chase Dekker/Shutterstock, 6-7; James Wheeler/Shutterstock, 8-9; Sergei Bachlakov/Shutterstock, 10; Anton Bielousov/Shutterstock, 11; almanino/Shutterstock, 12-13; Thomas Kurmeier/Getty, 14-15; julie deshaies/Shutterstock, 16; Armstrong Studios/Getty, 17; William Manning/Getty, 18-19; wojciech_gajda/iStock, 20-21; Eric Isselee/Shutterstock, 23.

Printed in the United States of America at Corporate Graphics in North Mankato, Minnesota.

TABLE OF CONTENTS

CHAPTER 1

WELCOME TO CANADA!

In what country can you find all four seasons at once? Where could you see a moose or bear in your backyard? Canada!

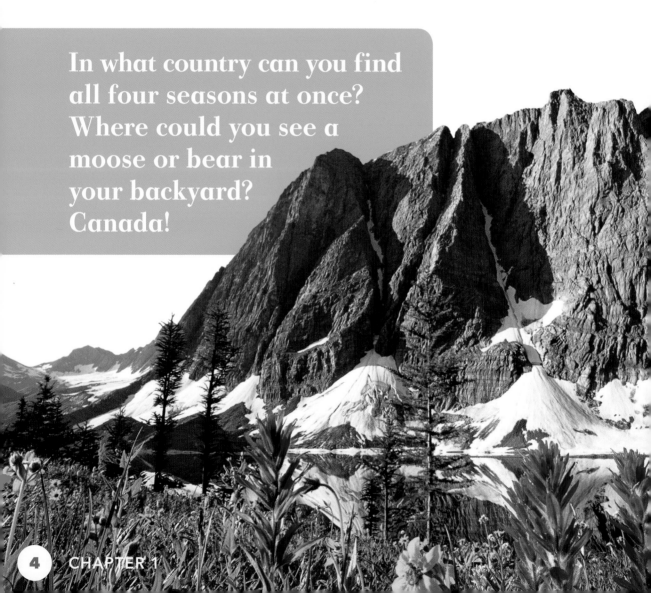

Caribou and Arctic wolves prowl the northern forests. Polar bears live near the Arctic Ocean.

caribou

Canada has large **plains**. Mountains loom in the west. There are many lakes and rivers. The frozen land in the north is called **tundra**. An **evergreen** forest divides it from the plains.

Summers can be warm or hot and humid. Winters are cold and snowy. West coast weather is rainy and mild.

DID YOU KNOW?

Canada is the second largest country in the world. Russia is the biggest.

lumber ·····▶

Canada has important **natural resources**. They are used for **exports**. What are they? Lumber. Oil. **Minerals**. Lumber is made into paper products. Oil becomes natural gas and petroleum. Mines produce coal, iron ore, stone, and metals.

Canada produces a lot of food. What kind? Farmers grow grain, fruit, and vegetables. They raise **livestock** for meat. Seafood is plentiful.

WHAT DO YOU THINK?

Canada has seven **climates**. How do you think that affects the country's natural resources?

CHAPTER 2

ONE COUNTRY, MANY WORLDS

Canada's citizens come from a lot of places. The country welcomes people of many other lands.

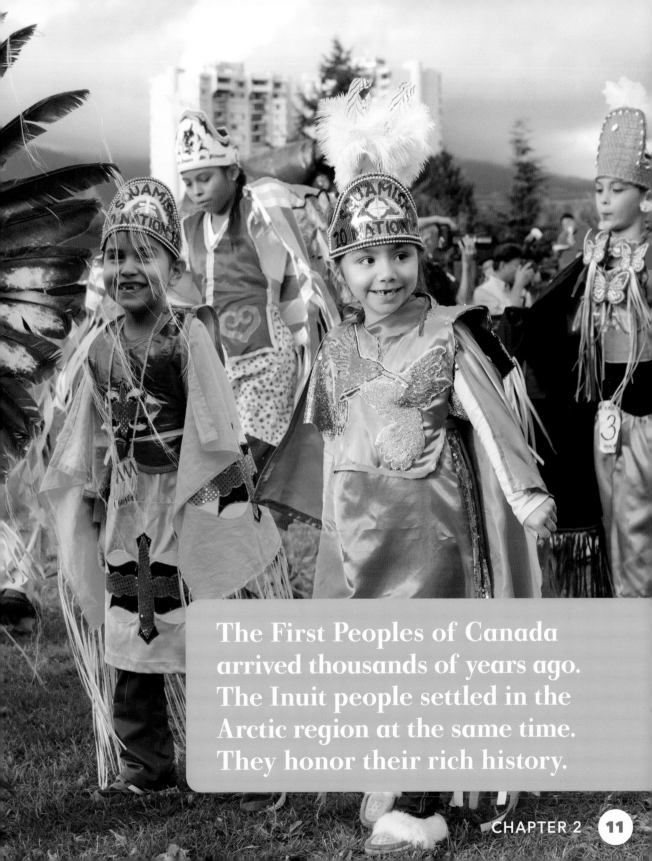

The First Peoples of Canada
arrived thousands of years ago.
The Inuit people settled in the
Arctic region at the same time.
They honor their rich history.

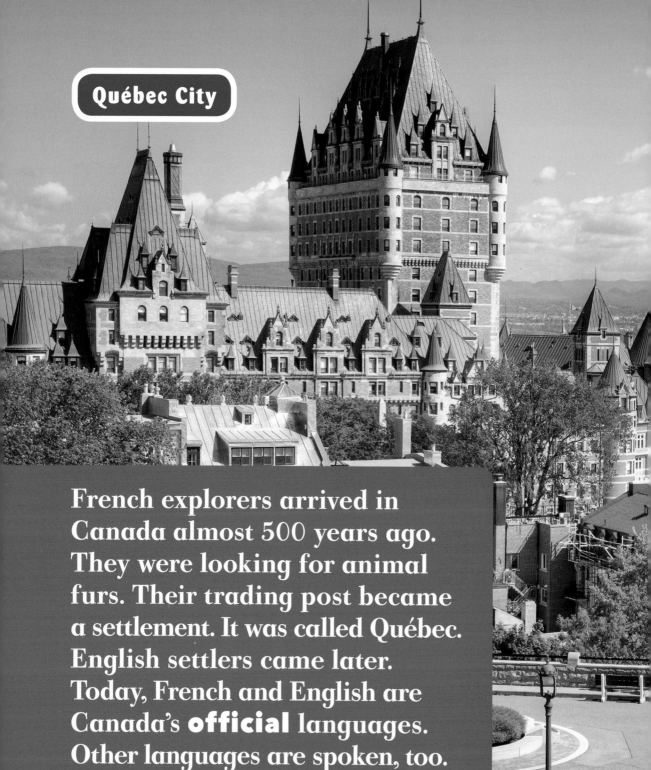

Québec City

French explorers arrived in Canada almost 500 years ago. They were looking for animal furs. Their trading post became a settlement. It was called Québec. English settlers came later. Today, French and English are Canada's **official** languages. Other languages are spoken, too.

TAKE A LOOK!

· ·

Québec is just one province. Canada has 10 provinces.
It also has three territories.

TERRITORIES:
① **Yukon**
② **Northwest Territories**
③ **Nunavut**

PROVINCES:
④ **British Columbia**
⑤ **Alberta**
⑥ **Saskatchewan**
⑦ **Manitoba**
⑧ **Ontario**
⑨ **Québec**

⑩ **Newfoundland and Labrador**
⑪ **New Brunswick**
⑫ **Nova Scotia**
⑬ **Prince Edward Island**

Canada became a country in 1867. Canada Day is celebrated on July 1. This is the date that it became a country. The holiday is celebrated with parades and fireworks.

DID YOU KNOW?

Québec is proud of its French roots. Québec National Day is celebrated on June 24. It is a day to celebrate French history.

CHAPTER 3

· ·

LIFE IN CANADA

Do you like French fries? What about gravy and melted cheese? If you do, you might like poutine. It is Canada's most famous dish.

poutine

What about maple syrup? It comes from Canada's maple trees.

The BRICK INVITATIONAL
SUPER NOVICE HOCKEY TOURNAMENT

WEST EDMONTON MALL

The BRICK

Most people live in cities in the south. They often take the bus or subway to work or school. Many have **service jobs**.

It is time for fun after work. Canadians like to play sports. Which one is their favorite? Hockey! Canada has more hockey players than any other country in the world.

WHAT DO YOU THINK?

Hockey is a big sport in Canada. Why do you think this is? What sports are popular where you live?

Fun happens all year. Warm weather brings out the swimmers. They crowd the beaches. Hikers head for the mountains. Outdoor fairs draw people with music, rides, and games.

In the winter, people bundle up to ski and skate. Some drill holes in frozen lakes to fish. What would you like to do in Canada?

QUICK FACTS & TOOLS

CANADA

Location: North America

Size: 3.9 million square miles
(10.1 million square kilometers)

Population: 35,623,680
(July 2017 estimate)

Capital: Ottawa

Type of Government:
federal parliamentary democracy
under a constitutional monarchy

Languages: English and French

Exports: cars, machinery, wood
products, oil, natural gas

GLOSSARY

caribou: Large animals in the deer family.

climates: The weather typical of certain places over a long period of time.

evergreen: A bush or tree that has green leaves throughout the year.

exports: Products sold to different countries.

livestock: Animals that are kept or raised on a farm or ranch.

minerals: Naturally occurring substances obtained from the ground, usually for humans to use.

natural resources: Materials produced by the earth that are necessary or useful to people.

official: Having the approval of an authority or public body.

plains: Large, flat areas of land.

service jobs: Jobs and work that provide services for others, such as hotel, restaurant, and retail positions.

tundra: Frozen, treeless land. The layer below it is permafrost, or land that will never thaw.

INDEX

TO LEARN MORE

Learning more is as easy as 1, 2, 3.

1) Go to www.factsurfer.com
2) Enter "Canada" into the search box.
3) Click the "Surf" button to see a list of websites.

With factsurfer, finding more information is just a click away.